THE BLUEBELL RAILWAY

MATT ALLEN

HALSGROVE

First published in Great Britain in 2008

Copyright © Matt Allen 2008

British Library Cataloguing-in-Publication Data
A CIP record for this title is available from the British Library

ISBN 978 1 84114 708 6

HALSGROVE
Halsgrove House,
Ryelands Industrial Estate,
Bagley Road, Wellington, Somerset TA21 9PZ
Tel: 01823 653777 Fax: 01823 216796
email: sales@halsgrove.com
website: www.halsgrove.com

Printed and bound by Grafiche Flaminia, Italy

INTRODUCTION

In this book, Halsgrove's Railway series takes us to rural Sussex and the magnificent Bluebell Railway. The Railway, mainly run by volunteers operates steam train services between Sheffield Park and Kingscote in Sussex. It is one of the county's biggest tourist attractions with over 180,000 visitors per year and is also one of the major Heritage Railways in the UK, providing a home for a great selection of essentially 'Southern' locomotives and rolling stock. The Bluebell is unique in being the only 'All Steam' railway in the UK where the dawn of the diesel is an alien concept!

This book will take you on a journey along the 9-mile line, with the seasons coming and going along the route. We can see magnificently restored steam locomotives and rolling stock, the authentic stations, the special events that the railway holds each year and, of course, the people who make it all possible.

Originally the Bluebell Railway was a part of the Lewes to East Grinstead Railway. The L&EGR, as it was known, was initially promoted in 1876, the chairman of the L&EGR being the Earl of Sheffield who owned Sheffield Park. However, the project didn't get off the ground until the L&EGR approached the London and Brighton South Coast Railway for assistance in 1878. On 1 Aug 1882 the line from Lewes to East Grinstead was opened, primarily intended for freight use. After all, it was promoted as a 'landowner's line' and, running through one of the most rural areas in Sussex, passengers were a secondary concern. In addition to the line from Lewes to East Grinstead, there was also a spur that connected Horsted Keynes to Ardingly and Haywards Heath, opened on 3 Sept 1883. The Southern Railway absorbed the whole line in 1923, but by this time the decline had set in and, like many rural lines, the march of the motor car was taking its toll on passenger numbers and freight traffic alike. Initially, financial saving was made by closure of signal boxes and then the running down of the railway's infrastructure.

Under nationalisation, British Railways took over in 1948 and by the early 1950s plans for the line's closure – it was an unremunerative branch line – were being drawn up. Posters advertising 'Closing of the East Grinstead-Lewes Line' appeared with the demise to occur on 13 June 1955, although with a national footplatemen's strike closure occurred on 28 May 1955. However, following representations by a local resident, Miss Madge Bessemer, it was discovered the closure was illegal due to the original Act of Parliament, requiring four trains to run each day, sadly only calling at selected stations. The doughty Miss Bessemer, granddaughter of Sir Henry Bessemer whose name is perpetuated in the Bessemer steel making process, won the day and the line reopened on 7 August 1956. However, after a public enquiry held in Lewes in

October 1957, the legal constraints were overcome by British Railways and on 16 March 1958 the line closed for a second and final time.

On 24 December 1959, a group of volunteers, keen not to see the line disappear into history, were able to lease the 4½ mile section of line from Sheffield Park to the south of Horsted Keynes under a five year term. In 1960 the idea of a preserved railway was a new concept, with those involved being in reality the pioneers of the railway preservation movement. The Bluebell, a nickname that stuck with the line due to the great display of flowers in springtime, provided a base for the rapidly disappearing steam locomotive. Historical accuracy was to the forefront of what they were trying to achieve; I wonder if they could imagine, or even hope, that it would turn into the wonderful railway it is today.

The first items of rolling stock began to arrive on 17 May 1960 with the first trains running for the newly formed 'Bluebell Railway Ltd' on 7 August 1960. In 1967 a huge step forward was made when the lease of the line was converted into an outright purchase, completed the following year. During the early years the railway continued to build up an almost unrivalled collection of locomotives and rolling stock as well as renovating and improving the infrastructure.

The Bluebell Railway always had an eye on extension – although extending south from Sheffield Park would have been very difficult as a bridge had been removed. The spur from Horsted Kenyes to Haywards Heath was also ruled out, certainly in the short to medium term, as a viaduct just west of Horsted Keynes had been demolished. An extension north through West Hoathly to Kingscote and East Grinstead seemed the best option. Gradually, after a public enquiry in 1983, negotiations with local landowners and the acquisition of the land and stations the railway moved north. By 1992 trains were running through West Hoathley tunnel, the longest tunnel on any heritage railway in the UK, for the first time with the former station site at West Hoathly being a temporary terminus although passengers could not alight from trains there. 1994 saw the service extended to Kingscote, which had been purchased and renovated, including the rebuilding of the down platform and buildings. This is not the end of the story as plans to extend north from Kingscote to East Grinstead are at an advanced stage with the achievement of being reconnected to the national network at East Grinstead on the horizon.

To me, the Bluebell today manages to capture the atmosphere of a steam era railway unparalleled by any other line I've visited. Perhaps it's the array of locomotives and rolling stock that date from the late 1880s right up to the twilight of steam in the 1960s, or is it the authentically restored stations? Unfortunately I'm not old enough to have experienced steam in British Railways' style but a trip to the Bluebell gives me an insight as to what I imagine it to have been like.

If you haven't paid a visit to the Railway, hopefully this book will convince you that a visit is a must. Maybe try one of the special events held throughout the year, the fabulous Pullman dining trains or just a trip along the line on a lovely summer's day.

I'd like to thank the friends who have helped me with this book, your input has been most appreciated.

This book is dedicated to my wife Katie who puts up with a lot of railway trips and holidays: the book wouldn't have been possible without her patience and support.

Matt Allen
Basingstoke,
December 2007

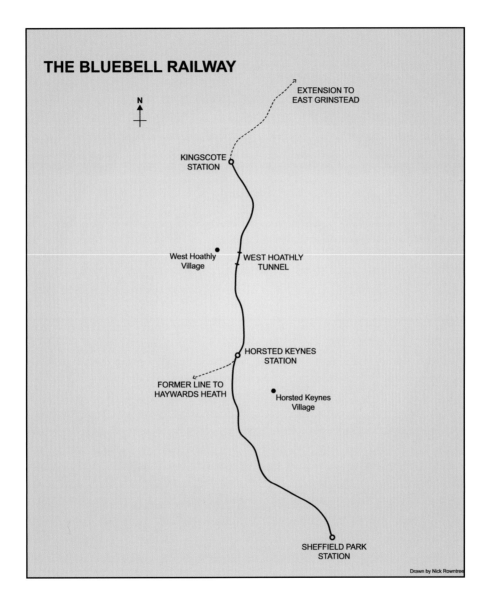

THE BLUEBELL RAILWAY

N

EXTENSION TO
EAST GRINSTEAD

KINGSCOTE
STATION

West Hoathly
Village

WEST HOATHLY
TUNNEL

HORSTED KEYNES
STATION

FORMER LINE TO
HAYWARDS HEATH

Horsted Keynes
Village

SHEFFIELD PARK
STATION

Drawn by Nick Rowntree

The journey begins. When the line was originally opened as the Lewes to East Grinstead Railway in 1882 Sheffield Park was an intermediate station on the line, but is now the starting point for the 9-mile journey to Kingscote. Here 01 class locomotive, No. 65 built in 1896 and subsequently rebuilt in 1908, complete with coaches dating from1922 is ready to depart with a late afternoon 'Vintage Train'.

The station with all its original features is a rail fan's dream. A great place to spend a few hours looking around the engine sheds, take a look at the museum on platform two, maybe have a meal in the Bessemer Arms or simply sit and watch the trains come and go.

Vintage signs make Sheffield Park Station a great place to explore, presenting opportunities for different photographs. Here the lovely autumn light really brings the scene to life.

Opposite:
West Country class, No. 34100, *Appledore* (which is actually No. 34028, *Eddystone*, in disguise) sits in platform two during a photographers' special event. The Bluebell Railway is a very 'Photographer Friendly' place with various special photographic evenings and events through the year. The driver of the locomotive has been persuaded to pose for this evocative picture

The Railway holds numerous special events through the year, which normally have an intensive train service with trains leaving Sheffield Park every twenty five minutes or so. In this picture Sheffield Park is a busy place with the first train of 'The Giants of Steam' event getting ready to depart. The locomotive in view is West Country class, No. 21C123 *Blackmoor Vale*.

Opposite:
The overhaul of operational locomotives and the restoration of longer term projects all take place in the works adjacent to Sheffield Park Station. Here, two 'non operational' locomotives are seen in the yard during a specially arranged photoshoot. The locomotives are T9 class locomotive, number 120 and Schools class locomotive *Stowe* number 928.

Early morning and late evening sun is a photographer's friend, providing ideal light for photography.

Whilst the yard at Sheffield Park is out of bounds for safety reasons, there is a viewing area where you can see the locomotives being prepared and serviced. Here E4 class locomotive, No. 32473 has just had its fire cleaned after a day's work.

On platform two is a museum with an impressive array of artifacts and railway memorabilia.

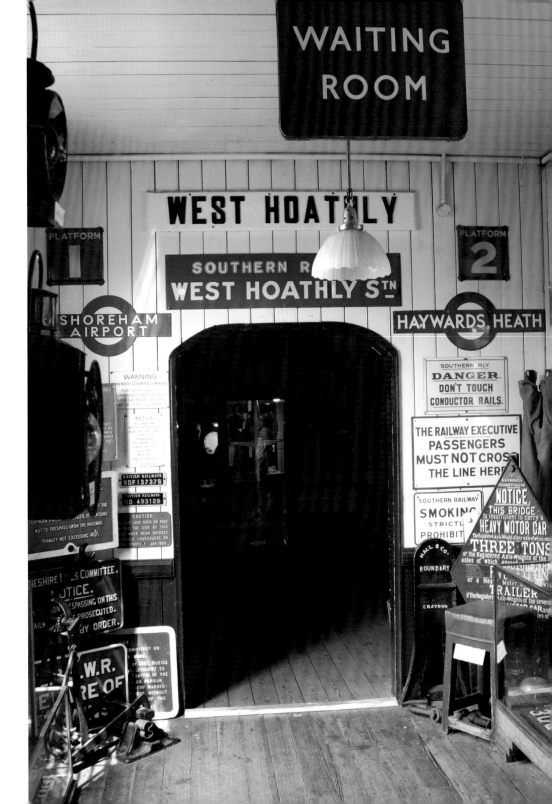

There are two main engine sheds at Sheffield Park which are adjacent to each other. The first, directly at the end of platform one, is used for storing locomotives that are awaiting a duty or an overhaul to return them to steam, under cover away from the elements. The second building, adjacent to the engine shed, is the main works where running repairs and major restoration projects are undertaken.

Amongst the collection of engines awaiting long term restoration are some real gems from the Southern Railway and its constituent companies. The two tank locomotives in view here are LSWR Adams Radial Tank, No.488, and South Eastern & Chatham Railway H Class Tank, No.263, both stored awaiting overhaul.

Here, T9 No. 120, which is a part of the National Collection, is seen outside the storage shed. This locomotive was last operational in 1993 but will hopefully return to steam in the future. The T9s were nicknamed *Greyhounds* on account of the turn of speed they could achieve.

Engine sheds and yards are always an ideal place to find different photographic angles or shots. Battle of Britain class, No. 34081, *92 Squadron*, based on the North Norfolk Railway was a visitor to the railway in 2007 for the annual 'Giants of Steam' event held each autumn.

Another visitor to the line was City class, No. 3440, City *of Truro*. Seen here alongside another GWR locomotive, Dukedog class, No. 9017, *Earl of Berkeley,* from the Bluebell's home fleet. The visit of *City of Truro* was the first time both of these outside framed locomotives had been reunited in preservation. This picture definitely gives the impression that the GWR is performing a takeover in deep Southern territory!

Looking north towards Horsted Keynes on a quiet day, No. 80151 is waiting to depart from platform one whilst No. 9017 and a brake van sit in platform two.

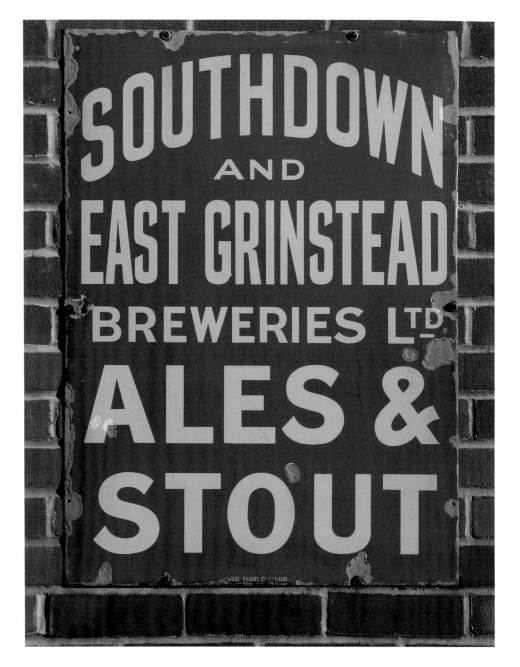

The Bessemer Arms is a purpose built pub and restaurant that was added to the station in 1986, although amazingly it looks an original structure. Southdown and East Grinstead Breweries were sold to Tamplins, a Brighton brewery, in 1924 for £274,000, but the sign gives an authentic feels to the Bessemer Arms. The pub's name commemorates Miss Madge Bessemer a local resident who fought against the closure of the Lewes to East Grinstead Railway in 1954.

An aerial view of the station taken from the footbridge. The footbridge was originally from Lingfield and was installed at Sheffield Park on 22 March 1985. The double width of the footbridge was to accommodate the race crowds at the adjacent racecourse at Lingfield Park. Sheffield Park is also the railway's administrative headquarters.

During the very popular 'War on the Line' event, the station is given some extra protection.

Christmas 'Pullman Style'. A Christmas dining train complete with original 1920s
Pullman carriages awaits its passengers at a festive Sheffield Park.

The line from Sheffield Park to Horsted Keynes is single track. After leaving the station it crosses Poleay bridge before beginning the journey to Horsted Keynes.

Opposite: There are some impressive signals just outside the station providing added interest. Access to take photographs from the lineside is possible if you have a 'lineside permit' and a 'high visibility jacket' both of which are available from the station. Getting up close to the action can provide some rewards; here No. 32473 makes a very spirited departure.

Close to the action again, with the station just visible in the background West Country class, No. 34100, *Appledore*, a renumbered and renamed No. 34028, climbs out of Sheffield Park towards the 1 in 75 gradient of Freshfield bank.

A classic 'Somerset and Dorset' combination, BR Standard class 4 locomotive,
No. 75027, pilots West Country class No. 34028, *Eddystone*.

Reputed to be the first steam locomotive to reach 100mph, No. 3440, *City of Truro* was at the Railway for two weeks during which it starred at the annual 'Giants of Steam' gala. Here the low autumn sun lights the engine perfectly. The locomotive is a part of the national collection and is always a popular visitor wherever it goes.

Another visitor for a 'Giants of Steam' in 2007 was West Country class No. 34007, *Wadebridge*. The 'Giants of Steam' event is held every autumn and gives the railway a chance to run an intensive service utilizing their larger locomotives usually supplemented by a visiting locomotive or two. No. 34007 returned to steam in October 2006 from ex Barry Scrapyard condition, the restoration being carried out at the Bodmin and Wenford Railway.

In soft autumnal light No. 34007 approaches Ketches Halt.

Opposite: After the departure from Sheffield Park the train begins the climb to Horsted Keynes. After crossing Poleay bridge the railway enters a cutting known as Ketches Lane, the site of a disused halt previously called Ketches Halt. In this picture on a hot summer's day, U Class No 1638 is making good work and immediately behind the locomotive is an LNWR Royal Saloon built in 1903. The Bluebell Railway has some very interesting and unique coaches, a number of which are illustrated here.

A great vintage sight. Another recently restored locomotive is C class, No. 592, here paired with a rake of Metropolitan Railway coaches having just rounded the curve at Ketches Lane and is onto Freshfield Bank. The Bluebell Railway has a collection of vintage coaches and matching locomotives that is unrivalled by any other Heritage Railway.

Opposite: Don't let anyone tell you Freshfield Bank is flat! Having walked up it many times I can vouch for that! This section of the Railway is a 1 in 75 climb towards Horsted Keynes and with open fields on both sides, presents plenty of photographic opportunities.

Another event that railway holds each year is the Goods Train weekend, giving the line a chance to return to its original roots since it was essentially built for freight traffic. U class, No. 1638, which is in the custodianship of the Maunsell Society, matches the SR goods wagons at the front of this impressive freight train.

Opposite: Dukedog, No. 9017 is seen getting into its stride on Freshfield Bank. The Bluebell is known for its impressive collection of Southern locomotives and rolling stock but this former Great Western locomotive is a very popular member of the home fleet. Ketches Halt is just out of sight as the track bears to the right at the bottom of the bank.

There's no better sight than a Bulleid pacific at speed. Here, No. 34100, a renamed No. 34028, heads a photographic charter. Despite the impression this pictures gives, in common with most Heritage Railways, the Bluebell runs under a Light Railway Order limiting speeds to 25mph.

No. 80151 coasts down Freshfield Bank with its train from Kingscote and Horsted Keynes. The engine is close to home, having originally been built at Brighton in 1956 at a cost of £21944, and being based at Brighton, Redhill and finally Eastleigh. Withdrawn from traffic in May 1967 and sold for scrap, after a mere eleven years in service, by British Railways in August 1967.

One of the home fleet of Bulleid Pacifics, No. 21C123, *Blackmoor Vale* hauls its train of
Pullman carriages towards Horsted Keynes early on a winter's morning. Photographs from this,
the east side of the line are unusual as lighting conditions for photography are difficult.

Further up Freshfield Bank this location is regular haunt for many photographers. *Blackmoor Vale* and U class
(otherwise known as the U boat) No. 1638, complement each other perfectly in their Southern Railway liveries.

This photograph catches a recreation of the last ever Golden Arrow boat train. This train was hauled by West Country class No. 34100, *Appledore,* with a green Bulleid coach at the head of the Pullman coaches and was recreated for a photographers' charter at the Bluebell. A number of photographers' charters are run at the Bluebell each year which enable unusual, but authentic, train combinations to be recreated.

Pictured at the annual branchline weekend held each spring, E4 class No. 32473, descends Freshfield Bank with a milk train complete with milk tank wagon behind the locomotive. The branchline event allows the smaller locomotives to get a workout. The railway carries around 200,000 visitors per year and the special events that are held contribute greatly to these numbers.

For this location on Freshfield Bank to prove successful for photography, blue skies are essential.

Not an easy technique, the panned shot can produce excellent results,
however these take a lot of practice and the failure rate is high.

Opposite: Every photograph has a story behind it. On this particular summer's day,
the weather forecast was great, so I thought I'd make the effort to travel to the
railway especially to photograph an evening Fish and Chip Special; unfortunately
the forecast didn't materialize. However, I was still pleased with the result,
the 1 in 75 climb is illustrated perfectly by No. 21C123, *Blackmoor Vale*.

A classic branchline freight with a distinctive Southern flavour being hauled by one of the diminutive Terrier locomotives. No. W8, *Freshwater*, visited the line from its home at the Isle of Wight Steam Railway. This engine dates back to 1876 and was built at Brighton Works; originally called *Newington*, numbered 46 but was later renumbered and renamed.

Battle of Britain class No. 34081, *92 Squadron*, in Brunswick green, makes an impressive sight on the climb to Horsted Keynes.

Canadian Pacific No. 35005 was a visitor to the railway and is seen here climbing Freshfield Bank. This Merchant Navy class locomotive has been used on the Mainline since preservation but is now based at the Mid Hants Railway.

During its first weekend back in service after a major overhaul the U boat, No. 1638, is seen with matching Southern Railway van and Maunsell coaches. Locomotives need to have a major overhaul and rebuild every ten years which can cost hundreds of thousands pounds.

Opposite: The Bluebell provides a great display of colours during the autumn, especially here at Broken bridge, so called because an occupation bridge was removed some time ago, although the supports remain. This is one of my favourite locations along the line, although the locomotives quite often shut off after reaching the top of Freshfield Bank so it can be a gamble as to whether they will be producing a steam effect. A legacy of the old bridge is an embankment which provides a great viewpoint to take pictures like this with BR Standard class 4, No. 75027, double heading with West Country class No. 34028, *Eddystone*.

No. 80151 comes through what remains of the bridge heading towards Sheffield Park;
the embankment frequented by photographers is to the left.

Terriers Top and Tail. The Branchline Gala weekends give the Railway chance to run different locomotive combinations, as seen here with No.662, *Martello*, on the front and home resident No. 672, *Fenchurch* on the rear – hence the Top and Tail.

City of Truro is still working hard as it approaches Broken bridge.

Golden Arrow dining trains are extremely popular with diners, running regularly through the year both in the daytime and the evening, giving dining passengers the chance to experience an on train restaurant experience Pullman style. The Railway has seven Pullman coaches some of which have been meticulously restored to their original condition as can be seen here with No. 75027 providing the motive power.

The Bluebell could not survive without the help of the many volunteers,
supplementing the relatively few paid staff, so sights like this take many
hours of volunteers' hard work to achieve.

Opposite: This photograph provides a great opportunity to compare the two different types of West Country class locomotives. No. 34007 at the front is in its original unrebuilt form with the air-smoothed casing, whilst No.34028 behind is in its rebuilt condition. The rebuilding of the class was designed to ease maintenance and reduce costs although their free running capabilities were never the same! The West Country class of locomotives are from the Bulleid pacific family, so called as they were designed by OVS Bulleid and had a pacific 4-6-2 wheel arrangement: they are identical to the Battle of Britain class of locomotives. Both are referred to as light pacifics, whilst their big brothers are the more powerful Merchant Navy class.

A visit of E Class, Metropolitan Railway, No. 1, based at the Buckinghamshire Railway Centre provided a great opportunity for an original Metropolitan Railway formation, as seen here passing through Broken bridge. This locomotive was built in 1898 and the coaches in 1900 and scenes like this would have been commonplace on the Chesham branch in Metro Land, referring to the Metropolitan Railway's route.

Sunshine and showers can give some great lighting conditions. With sunshine and angry skies No. 80151 is seen heading south towards Sheffield Park. Very few engines face south, in fact in photographs in this book only Nos. 80151, 32473 and No. 672, *Fenchurch* are seen facing south. With no turntable on the Bluebell, locomotives can only be turned using a low loader lorry, only really possible if the locomotive visits another line requiring road transport.

A lovely summer's evening with a great 'glint' on the side of No. 34021, *Dartmoor*, in reality No. 34028, *Eddystone*, in disguise. The glint photograph, where the light causes a lovely shimmer on the side of the locomotive, is the holy grail in railway photography terms requiring the sun to be low and at the correct angle.

Opposite: Moving north towards Horsted Keynes this shot is taken at Rock Cutting, with the early morning light creating a great effect.

One of the home based Terriers, officially known as an A1 class, No. 672, *Fenchurch*, is seen at Tremains with a short freight during the Goods Train weekend held each spring. *Fenchurch* was built to an LBSCR Stroudley design in 1872.

No. 80151 with a mixed rake of BR Mk1 and Maunsell coaches rounds the curve at Tremains.

Bulleid Power steaming through Sussex....a lovely autumnal scene. The Bulleid pacifics, which includes the West Country, Battle of Britain and more powerful Merchant Navy classes, were stalwarts of the Southern Railway and Southern Region from the 1940s until the end of Southern steam in July 1967. The Bulleid pacifics were a rare sight on what is now the Bluebell with only the original West Country and Battle of Britain classes putting in an appearance.

Back at the whistle board where we previously saw *Fenchurch*, the Standard tank is employed on Pullman duties with the lunchtime Golden Arrow. The railway normally uses one of the larger tender locomotives on the Golden Arrow for authenticity, although the Standard tank is more than up to the task.

C class No. 592, resplendent in its freshly applied South East and Chatham
Railway Livery, makes its way through Lindfield wood in lovely winter sunshine.
Lindfield wood changes dramatically through the seasons making it an ideal
place for photographs in contrasting conditions.

The Golden Arrow heads through Lindfield Wood on Sunday lunchtime with a Pullman train; I could almost smell the roast dinners as they went past! No. 34028, *Eddystone* was restored to steam at the Swanage Railway but has been on hire to the Bluebell Railway.

Opposite: Any book on the Bluebell wouldn't be complete without a photograph to illustrate how it got its nickname. Lindfield wood is one of the best places on the line to see the wonderful display of spring flowers.

The Dukedog makes its way northbound during a busy Gala weekend. No. 9017 is one of the locomotives nicknamed Dukedogs since they were an amalgamation of parts from the Bulldog and a Duke classes; the parts of this engine are thus actually older than the 'building' date suggests. The 1938 rebuild of No. 9017, actually No. 3217 at that time, used the frames from Bulldog, No. 3425, built 1906, and boiler and cab from Duke class, No. 3282, originally named *Chepstow Castle* and built in 1899.

This may look like a Swiss snowblower, but in fact it is No. 34081, *92 Squadron*,
seen early one morning at Holywell, on the approach to Horsted Keynes.

Holywell is a location where you can photograph in both directions; in this photograph No. 32473 is seen heading south. You can park very close to the line here where the road passes under the railway, which isn't always the case at the Bluebell. I wouldn't like to count how many miles I've walked up and the down the lineside!

Taken from the top of the bridge seen in the previous picture No. 1638 heads a demonstration freight train towards Horsted Keynes. Whilst the wagons are no longer used for revenue earning service, they contribute greatly to the atmosphere and authenticity of the line, having a workout on photographers' specials and gala events.

No. 80151, one of the resident Standard tanks, so called as they were built to a BR Standard design, steams through Holywell, with Keysford road bridge in view, giving a pleasant view of the Sussex countryside.

Double-headed unrebuilt Bulleid pacifics or Spam Cans as they are affectionately known, with *Blackmoor Vale* from the home fleet and visitor *Wadebridge*. This photograph was taken at the 2007 Giants of Steam Gala which was a Bulleid bonanza with no less than four Bulleid pacifics in steam.

Blackmoor Vale is seen crossing Keysford bridge. The coach at the rear of this train is an LNWR saloon that was built in 1913, running in BR days between Llandudno and Blaenau Ffestiniog. For a supplementary fare you can now travel in this coach at the Bluebell giving panoramic views of your journey.

True Giants of Steam in the form of double-headed Bulleid pacifics; this time a Battle of Britain class locomotive, No. 34081, *92 Squadron* and West Country class No. 34028, *Eddystone*. Running double-headed combinations is always popular with enthusiasts at the special events held throughout the year.

Photographed in the same location as the previous picture but from the other side of the line. The goods van directly behind *Blackmooe Vale* is of interest being a steam heated banana van, designed to ensure the fruit didn't spoil and continued to ripen. This particular van, No. 750027 was built by the LMS in 1946 and purchased by the Railway in 1965.

E4, No. 32473, is seen here returning to Sheffield Park from Horsted Keynes after a day's work on a Driving and Firing Course, where people can experience a day on the footplate.
The bridge you can see in distance is Three Arch bridge which is just south of Horsted Keynes.

No. 34100, *Appledore,* breaks into the sunlight as it leaves the cutting on the approach to Three Arch bridge.

Three Arch bridge is one of the main landmarks on the Bluebell and is an ideal place for railway photography. The locomotives are normally working hard as they come under the bridge as the gradient is 1 in 75, the same as Freshfield Bank, and the regulator is shut off shortly afterwards as they approach Horsted Keynes. In this photograph No. 65 is paired with the wooden-bodied Metropolitan coaches.

Taken through Three Arch bridge on a summer's day, No. 32473 is returning to Sheffield Park.

Bluebells predominate here, as at Lindfield wood,
as the Standard tank No. 80151 comes under the bridge.

No. 34007 makes a great spectacle coming under Three Arch bridge.

Opposite: Bluebell-based No. 32473 pilots Ivatt 2MT, No. 41312 a visitor
from the Mid Hants Railway with both locomotives in matching BR black livery.
75A on the smokebox of No. 32473 indicates it was allocated to Brighton
shed or motive power depot so is on home territory at the Bluebell.

After Three Arch bridge, the railway opens out with fields on either side of the line for the approach to Horsted Keynes station. This provides some great photographic opportunities especially when the sun is low in sky as seen in this picture. The sheep seem totally unconcerned that years of history are rolling past them!

No. W8, *Freshwater*, is seen approaching Horsted Keynes with a short freight train. The locomotive is dwarfed by the wagon behind and also the fireman who looks huge in comparison to the locomotive.

With Three Arch bridge just visible in the background No. 34021, (No. 34028 in another disguise!) makes its approach to Horsted Keynes.

Fenchurch complete with Metropolitan coaches makes a real historic train. The coaches have to be seen up close to fully appreciate the skill and detail in their restoration.

Taken from the opposite side of the line to the previous picture, a light pacific, No. 34028, is silhouetted perfectly. There are only a couple of locations along the line where a silhouette is possible, this location probably being the best. The Bluebell operates trains for approximately three hundred days a year, so there is plenty of opportunity to make the most of the changing light throughout the year. Travelling on a steam train when it is dark is an amazing experience!

Stepney, No. 572, another of the home based Terriers looks tiny in comparison with No. 65, the contrasting liveries creating a real splash of colour. *Stepney* cost £750 when purchased from BR – with a couple of coaches thrown in – in 1960.

No. 1638 at the helm for Golden Arrow duties, with a lovely autumn backdrop. When the dining train runs at lunchtime it normally completes two round trips of the line, giving the passengers plenty of time to eat their meal.

The sign at a foot crossing just south of Horsted Keynes makes things
perfectly clear as No. 9017 rolls past. Note the fireman drinking his tea!

Opposite: The City Limited is a breakfast Pullman train that is run a couple of times a year. In this photo
you can see the fields either side of the line, the location of the previous pictures. The bridge over
the road is New Road bridge, where, during special events, you will see the photographers' cars parked!

Doubled headed Spam Cans. *92 Squadron* and *Wadebridge* catch the low sun perfectly during the 2007 Giants of Steam event, when both these locomotives were visiting the line for this special occasion. As the Bluebell doesn't have a main line connection, which will hopefully change with the East Grinstead extension, any visiting locomotives are brought in by road on low loaders.

This picture is really taken at the Bluebell despite a Great Western double header and a Great Western liveried coach behind the locomotives! The pairing of Nos. 3440 and 9017 was something that had been long awaited by railway enthusiasts, as they are the sole remaining outside-framed GWR locomotives. When this picture was taken there were at least seventy photographers in the field to record the occasion.

Making sights and sounds like this possible lands the Railway with an annual coal bill of approximately £160,000. 34100 puts on a fine display on the approach to Horsted Keynes.

A busy scene at Horsted Keynes. No. 75027 is arriving with a train from Sheffield Park, No. 80154, a renumbered No. 80151, is waiting to depart and the signalman is dealing with the token exchange all in a torrential downpour.

Horsted Keynes station, with period cars during a War on the Line event, complete with masking tape on the windows. Stations on the Bluebell all follow a similar design and are rather grand in nature with Horsted Keynes being restored to the 1930s' Southern Railway period.

The station at Horsted Keynes is approximately a mile from the centre of village, which wasn't so much of a problem in the early days as the line was built essentially for freight traffic. However, as the popularity of the motor car spread, the distance of the station didn't help matters and the decline set in.

Metropolitan No. 1 climbs away from Horsted Keynes heading for Kingscote on a lovely summer's evening. The Chesham coaches pictured were originally purchased by the Bluebell from London Transport at a cost of £260. Now fully restored their value has increased somewhat!

Sunset in Sussex. Looking towards Sheffield Park from the south end of Horsted Keynes, you can see the carriage and wagon works on the left hand side. All the restoration and maintenance work on coaches and wagons is carried out here, whilst rolling stock awaiting longer term storage can be seen behind the far right-hand platform.

Inside the carriage works is a viewing platform allowing the public to see the work in process.
It's worth bearing in mind that much of the work is carried out by volunteers.

No. 32473 sits between platforms four and five with a milk train for Sheffield Park during
a photographers' night shoot. The Railway utilises the photographers' market very successfully
and stages a number of similar events throughout the year.

The station at Horsted Keynes is an elaborate affair with five platforms, complete with underpasses to get between each platform. It has the appearance of a London suburban station and not one of a village in rural Sussex and is an interesting place to explore, packed with original features. Two visiting locomotives Ivatt, No. 41312 and Merchant Navy class, No. 35005, both visiting from the Mid Hants Railway, are seen on a cold winter's evening.

Terrier, No. W8, with a short freight train pauses at Horsted Keynes, giving the driver opportunity to change the lamp.

On the opposite side of the station to the previous picture Nos. 34028 and 75027 wait in torrential rain; note the fact the locomotives are using lamps and not discs to display the head codes.

No. 80151 is heading south from Horsted Keynes with the Golden Arrow and judging by the people on the platform there is a special event on at the time. One of the carriage repair sheds can be seen on the right.

Sir Berkeley, seen here at Horsted Keynes, was built by Manning Wardle & Company at their Boyne Engine Works in Leeds in 1890 and visited the Bluebell for its 125th anniversary. A sister engine, *Sharpthorne*, which is a static exhibit on the line, was used in the building of the line, so it seemed a fitting visitor for the occasion.

Over 30,000 of these Mechanical Horses, of varying designs and manufacturers, were produced. They are quite often visitors to the Railway adding to the period atmosphere. Here, an ex-British Railways Scarab is seen on the platform.

The E4, complete with LMS van, has the signal and pulls away towards the station at Horsted Keynes. Out of view on this picture is the spur that used to run to Ardingly and Haywards Heath. Hopefully, one day the section of line maybe re-opened and, in the meantime, it provides further storage space for rolling stock.

No. 34100, *Appledore* is seen pulling into Horsted Keynes and is about to leave the single track and enter the station section. With five platforms the signaling and track arrangements are quite complex. The branch to Ardingly and Haywards Heath is just out of sight behind the trees.

A timeless, almost 1960s' scene at Horsted Keynes.

Horsted Keynes is an ideal place to spend a few hours watching trains arrive and depart. Wherever you turn there are authentic features, fitting in with the Southern Railway period of the station.

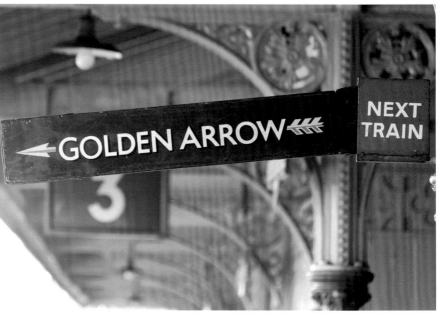

The next train at platform three is the Golden Arrow.

West Country vs Terrier is a rather unfair race! Leamland bridge, just north of the
station is an ideal venue for a good view of the entire station site.

The station staff are doubling up as Home Guard, at least for the duration of a Southern at War weekend.

There is a large field adjacent to the station site which doubles up as a car park or special events field. During the 125th Anniversary of the opening of the line, the field was transformed into a period funfair, complete with traction engines.

Night photography is one of my favourite types of railway photography. It seems to capture a different atmosphere of a bygone age, seen here with No. 34028, *Eddystone*.

Another feature of the 125th Anniversary celebrations was a run past of all the engines in traffic over the celebration weekend. The cavalcade is seen here running through the station with Nos. 55, 672, 9017, 65, 32473, 1638, 34028 and 21C123. I wonder how many hours of restoration went into all those locomotives?

Bulleid heaven. Visitors, *Wadebridge*, from the Mid Hants Railway and *92 Squadron*, from the North Norfolk Railway, are seen at Horsted Keynes.

Opposite: A one-off special event held at the Railway was a Terrier Gala. No. 32678 was a visitor from the Kent and East Sussex Railway for this special weekend and is seen here complete with some Bulleid coaching stock. Other visitors included No. W8, *Freshwater* and No. 662, *Martello* who were joined by No. 55, *Stepney* and No.672, *Fenchurch* from the home fleet.

No. 41312, although renumbered for this picture, under the signal box at the south end of Horsted Keynes Station.

Night Arrow. No. 21C123, which was numbered 34023 under the BR system, and was built at Brighton in 1946, complements the 1920s' Pullman coaches perfectly to create the ultimate Golden Arrow.

Night time at Horsted Keynes can be very atmospheric, with two unrebuilt Bulleids, Nos.34007 and 34081, waiting while a member of the crew looks on.

Grey skies don't necessarily mean I put the camera away! When the weather closes in station activities can provide the chance to take different photographs.

The Railway carries many different types of passengers, although I'm not sure what type of ticket Race Birds have to buy.

10.23 am and a pick up freight is waiting to leave Horsted Keynes. According to the chalking on the side of the banana van, its destination is Lingfield.

No. 34021, *Dartmoor* pulls away from the station in late summer sunshine. I wonder what OVS Bulleid would make of this scene with one of his locomotive designs and two of his coaches, attached directly behind the locomotive, still in service in 2007?

Looking through Leamland bridge back towards the station on a winter's day.

Coming under Leamland bridge, No. 34028 is starting the climb towards West Hoathly.
In this photograph you can see two tracks leading from the station site and converging,
just past Leamland bridge, into a single track that runs all the way to Kingscote.
In BR days the line from Kingscote to Horsted Keynes was double track.

Due to the geography of the line distant scenic shots are difficult. However just north of Horsted Keynes this vista of the Sussex countryside is possible. No. 1638 is heading a train towards Kingscote on what was a very cold winter's day.

In the same location as the previous photograph but taken from a closer field, No. 65 is getting up a good head of steam as it accelerates northwards. Between Christmas and New Year the Railway normally operates an all 'Vintage Train' service, so provides a great opportunity to see trains like this.

Next we come to Horsted House Farm, which is just north of the previous shot.
No. 80151 is seen here coasting toward Horsted Keynes with a Santa Special from Kingscote.
Christmas is always a very busy time on the line with an intensive service of Santa Specials.

Opposite: 672 is heading a southbound train towards
Leamland bridge on a lovely winter's day.

A lovely South East and Chatham Railway scene with No. 65, in SE&CR livery and two of the SE&CR Hundred Seater coaches directly behind the engine. These coaches are referred to as Hundred Seaters as they have ten passenger compartments which can each seat ten people. These where built in 1922 and came to the Bluebell in 1963.

Still on the climb towards West Hoathly tunnel, we see Nos. 75027 and 34028 at Black Hut on a very autumnal day. This part of the line is normally out of bounds to photographers, but a special photographers' charter provided a chance to use this location.

No. 5690, *Leander* adds a splash of colour on a rather grey day. The Jubilee class locomotive, which was a visitor, has just left the West Hoathly tunnel at the head of a Wizard Express and is heading for Kingscote. The pumpkins on the front of the locomotive, indicate it is Halloween, when the railway runs the special Wizard Weekend, a great attraction for the younger visitor.

With a length of 731 yards, West Hoathly tunnel is the longest on a preserved railway in the UK and is also on a steep gradient. No. 41302, actually No. 41312 from the Mid Hants Railway, is working hard on its journey to Kingscote. This part of the line will be familiar to anyone who has watched the film *The Railway Children*, filmed in 1999. The Railway is regularly used as a television and film set.

Adjacent to the tunnel is the site of the former West Hoathly Station, the brick fronts of the platforms still being visible. The Standard tank is heading for the tunnel with a train from Kingscote. These engines were found all over the BR system due to their versatility, with 154 being built at Brighton, Derby and Doncaster works between 1951 and 1956.

On a hot summer's day, *Blackmoor Vale* makes a great sight in its Southern livery. This locomotive is owned by the Bulleid Society. Sister locomotive, rebuilt Battle of Britain class Bulleid pacific, No. 34059, *Sir Archibald Sinclair,* is currently under restoration at Sheffield Park.

No. 21C123 at the head of the famous Atlantic Coast Express
which seems to have been diverted via rural Sussex on its way to
the West Country from Waterloo! Special events at the Railway
allow for unusual headboards, with locomotives being
temporarily renumbered and renamed for added interest.

Winter frost and sunshine paint this location, literally in a totally different light!

It's 2.5 miles from the tunnel to Kingscote with much of this being a tree-lined cutting. The E4 tank is seen heading a southbound train near Birch Farm crossing with recent line side clearance in evidence. This locomotive is the sole survivor of its type, being designed by Robert Billinton and built at Brighton works in 1898.

A completely contrasting photograph, the same locomotive and the same bridge, the difference between summer and winter is all too clear. The Golden Arrow, seen here, has three 1920s' vintage Pullman coaches *Fingall, Lilian* and *Christine* and a 1960s' Metro Cammell-built Pullman coach, *Eagle*.

Opposite: The U boat, No. 1638, is seen rolling down the gradient towards Kingscote with a Santa Special. The bridge in the background is at Mill Place.

Again the difference between summer and winter. In the summer this photograph isn't possible due the vegetation that grows obscuring the view. In fact I've walked past this location in the summer and not given it a second look.

The speed limit approaching Kingscote signal box and station is 10 mph.

Justt as the train approaches Kingscote Station, there is a small signal box that controls operations. As the driver of *Fenchurch* leans out to hand over the signal token you can see the beginning of the double track station section. Kingscote Station had been used as a private residence so required complete renovation when the Railway purchased it in 1985.

A grey day at Kingscote with No. 80151 waiting to leave with a Sheffield Park train. The station was built in 1882, and now reflects its 1950s' BR style. Currently it is the northern terminus of the line, although the 2-mile extension north to East Grinstead and a connection back with the Network Rail mainline is at an advanced stage.

In this photograph, the E4 has made the signal token exchange and is approaching the station.

A great BR era train, with the Standard tank and Mark I coaches heading south from Kingscote.

The Bluebell is a single track railway and trains can only pass in the stations as seen here. The E4 is heading towards a very quiet Kingscote whilst *Fenchurch* waits to depart. There are no car parking facilities at Kingscote but there is a regular, and sometimes vintage, bus connection to East Grinstead.

Following on from the previous picture, the E4 is now at the station with its passengers spilling onto the platform whilst the Terrier makes a spirited departure. These tiny locomotives are always popular with their distinctive sound and the characteristic smoke effects they produce.

Nearly but not quite! The extension north to East Grinstead has been a lengthy and costly affair, but is now in sight. With no fewer than twelve landowners to be negotiated with and Imberhorne tip to be cleared it truly has been a mammoth project. The final planning permission has now been granted and the dream is definitely going to become reality.

The Bluebell Railway's moto is 'Floreat Vapour' which translates to 'Let Steam Flourish', something which sums up this delightful line perfectly. I hope you enjoyed the journey.